A Senior Moment
is just a
Wrinkle
in Time

prayers, sayings and chuckles

Inspired by Faith

Senior Moment
©Product Concept Mfg., Inc.

One great thing
about getting older-

Your old meaningless
stuff is now
"retro" and worth
a lot of money.

Grow old
with me!
The best
is yet to be.

- Robert Browning

A Senior Moment is just a Wrinkle in Time

Wrinkles
should merely
indicate
where smiles have been.

– Mark Twain

• • • • • • • • • •

*May this little book
bring new smiles to your face,
and a lift to your heart.*

Prayer for
Aging Gracefully

• • • • • • • • • • •

Create in me a happy heart,
preserve my memory safe and sound—
May all my aches be little ones,
and let the things I lose be found.
Send me, I pray, my daily smiles,
a serving, too, of prunes and bran—
Help me accept my graying hair,
and keep the most of it I can.
Remind me to forgive myself
when senior moments come along—
Provide a time for exercise
so these old bones stay fit and strong.
Lord, keep my attitude upbeat,
and free from worry, cares and fears—
Each day, help me appreciate
the gift and goodness of my years.
Amen.

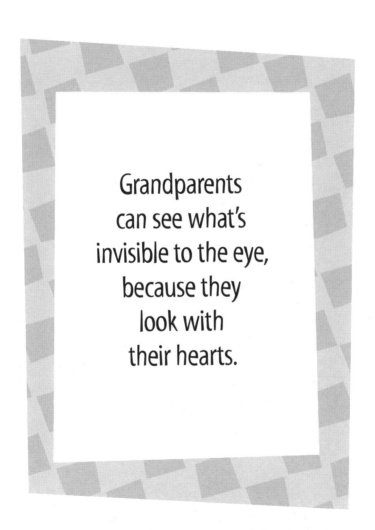

Grandparents
can see what's
invisible to the eye,
because they
look with
their hearts.

I've heard they're
called
"laugh lines" –

Life sure is
funny,
isn't it!

The real act
of discovery
consists not in
finding new lands,
but in seeing
with new eyes.

-Marcel Proust

You've reached the age when...

- you feel more at home in antique shops than in electronic stores.
- you've bought a loaf of bread, a box of cereal, and a bag of marshmallows, and the bagger asks if you need help putting it in your car.
- you find yourself explaining to your friends what medications you're on and whether or not these medications are to be taken with food.
- your grandson earnestly asks you which of Jesus' disciples you used to hang around with.
- you ask to speak to the manager, and you find yourself complaining to someone no older than your last grandchild.
- a quiet evening at home is paradise, and you do everything you can to assure a quiet evening at home.
- you and your teeth sleep separately.
- they just don't make things like they used to.

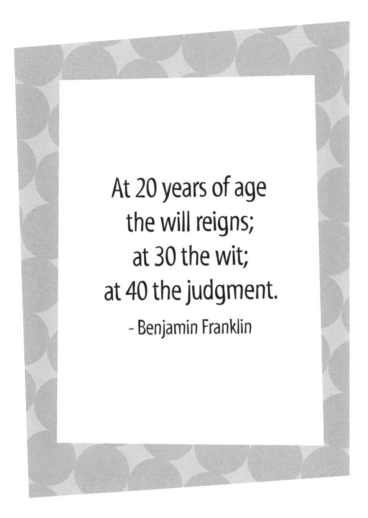

At 20 years of age
the will reigns;
at 30 the wit;
at 40 the judgment.

- Benjamin Franklin

There's a lot
to be said for
getting older...

But as my mother
always told me,
"If you can't say
something nice,
don't say anything
at all."

We can do
no great things.
Only small things
with great love.
- Mother Teresa

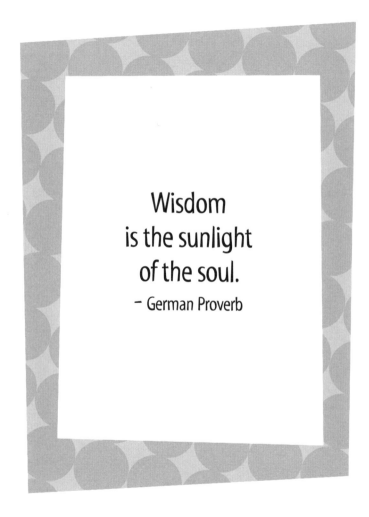

Wisdom
is the sunlight
of the soul.

− German Proverb

We
do not stop
playing
when we
grow old-

We grow old
when we stop
playing.

Getting together with old friends is about celebrating friendship, sharing laughter, making memories, exchanging advice and helpful tips...

(that is, catching up on the latest gossip.)

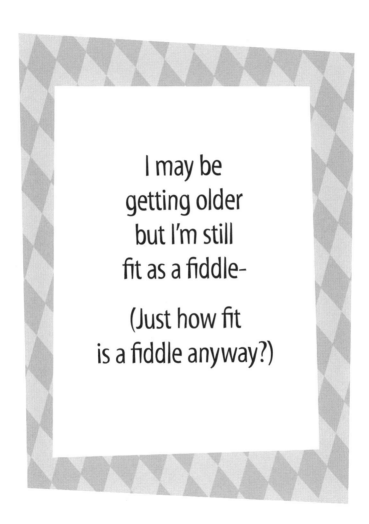

I may be
getting older
but I'm still
fit as a fiddle-

(Just how fit
is a fiddle anyway?)

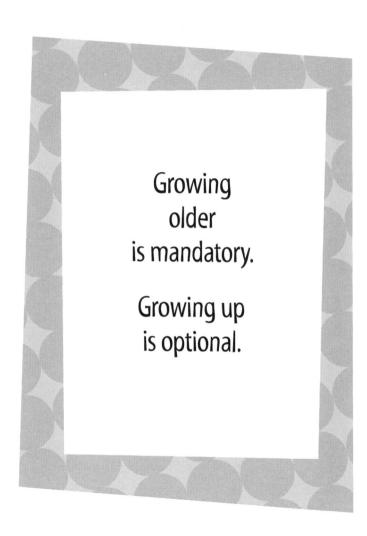

Growing
older
is mandatory.

Growing up
is optional.

Sometimes
you find your
very best friend
is right in your
own family.

Life's more fun
if you're cute...

You get away
with stuff.

Let me tell you
the best thing about
getting older!

As soon as I remember,
you'll be the
first person I tell.

A joyful
spirit is
always young.

Remember –
There is nothing
too big
(or too small)
to take to
the Lord.

No Tech-Knowledge-y Required

I'll never understand those phones
that buzz and beep and blink
And videos and all those cords
make me too confused to think.
In spite of what the kids say
I may never learn to text
or talk into computer-screens
or whatever trend comes next.
It seems a bit impersonal
to communicate by e-mail,
But I know just how to talk to God
cause I'm sure that He loves knee-mail.

God adores
the sound of
your voice-

Talk to him
often.

Fond memories
of times past
are keepsakes
of the heart.

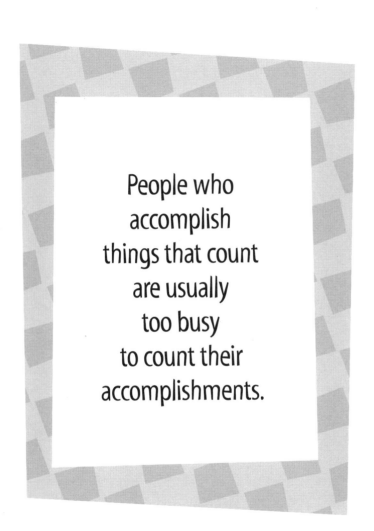

People who
accomplish
things that count
are usually
too busy
to count their
accomplishments.

Friends
are God's way
of smoothing out
the bumps
on the road
of life.

Lord, I remember when...
My clothes and hair were up-to-date,
I had the latest and the best.
I followed all the current trends,
and couldn't wait for what was next.

Yes, I remember when...
The most important things were bought
and shown with pride for all to see –
But now I've left those things behind
and, truth be told, I feel relieved.

Lord, I've discovered now...
It's what's inside the heart that counts,
the spirit's wealth that means the most.
Contentment, joy and thankfulness
are things I now hold dear and close.

Let patience, kindness, faith and love,
Forgiveness, laughter all increase!
Give me the time-worn, oldest gifts,
and most of all, a soul at peace.

It is one of the
blessings of old friends
that you can afford
to be stupid
with them.

- Ralph Waldo Emerson

Contemplating the Hereafter...

• • • • • • • • • •

The pastor came to visit one of his parishioners, a woman in her 90's and a shut-in. When the pastor inquired about her readiness for eternal life, the woman replied: "Yes, Pastor, I think about the hereafter all the time. I decide I want something from the kitchen, and by the time I get up from the chair, grab my cane, and make my way into the kitchen, I stand there wondering what in the world I'm here after."

The
"Top Ten List"
is not a
modern
invention.

A good laugh
is like manure
to a farmer–

it doesn't do
any good until
you spread it
around.

Never too old to learn.

- Latin proverb

During the first third of life,
everyone told you what to do.
During the second third of your
life, you told everyone
else what to do. During the
last third of your life,
everyone's telling you what
to do again.

The good thing is
you can't hear 'em,
so you don't care.

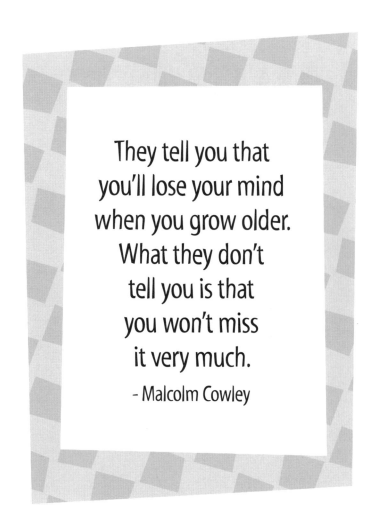

They tell you that
you'll lose your mind
when you grow older.
What they don't
tell you is that
you won't miss
it very much.

- Malcolm Cowley

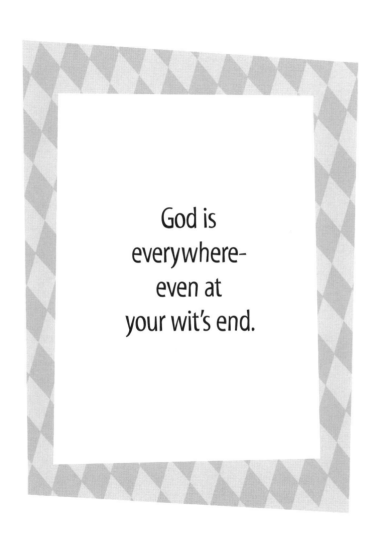

God is
everywhere-
even at
your wit's end.

Get your exercise today!

Walk with the Lord.

The bond
of friendship
is a blessing
that lasts
forever
in the heart.

When you're feeling stressed,
remember:
Moses started out
as a basket case,
and the Lord
made something
of him anyway!

WARNING:
Hair color is subject
to change
without notice.

The best mirror
is an old friend.

–George Herbert

A cheerful
heart is good
medicine.

– Prov. 17:22

Each morning,
God gives us a rose.
And some of us
will spend the day
complaining about
the thorns.

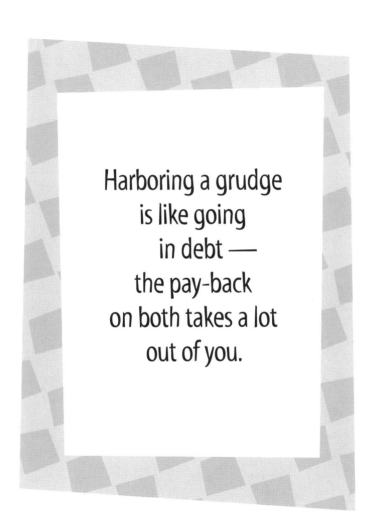

Harboring a grudge
is like going
in debt —
the pay-back
on both takes a lot
out of you.

Honey,
if you got it,
flaunt it.

Just be careful not to
throw your back out.

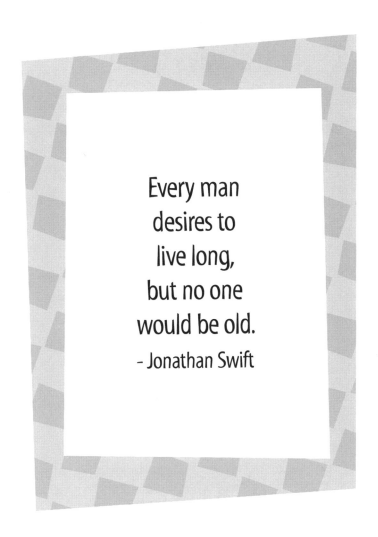

Every man
desires to
live long,
but no one
would be old.

- Jonathan Swift

12 ways to be Cantankerous

●　●　●　●　●　●　●　●　●　●　●

1. Decide you're tired of keeping it all in, and from now on you're going to tell everyone how you really feel. Then tell 'em.

2. If it walks, talks, or moves, blame it.

3. In the company of your adult children, repeat no family story less than 50 years old, preferably one that illustrates how insightful and smart you've always been as opposed to the insensitive boors you grew up with.

4. To any advice you know you should take but you don't want to hear, simply say, "You just don't understand," and stand your ground. Adamantly.

5. If it walks like a duck, looks like a duck, and quacks like a duck, call it an orangutan and insist you're right. Adamantly.

6. Don't let the fact you haven't heard the question stop you from answering it in no uncertain terms.

7. Sometime during every family celebration, announce that you probably won't be around for the next one, then gaze wistfully into the distance.

8. In the presence of your visitors, complain that you never have any visitors.

9. Within ear shot of the person who drives you to and from your doctors' appointments, inform others that no one ever does anything for you.

10. Never settle for a simple request when an angry rant will do.

11. When you receive a gift, put it away and explain to the sender that you're "saving it for good."

12. If they don't laugh at your jokes, it's because they don't have a sense of humor, and it's high time you point this out (see tip #1).

• • • • • • • • • •

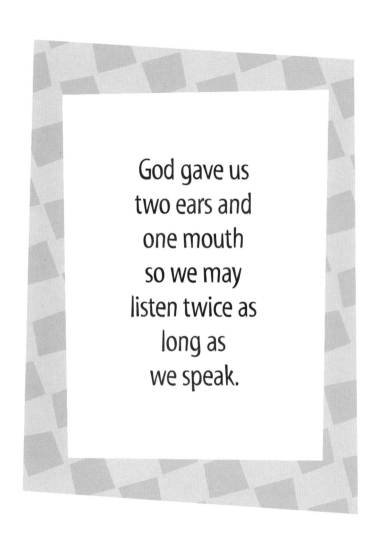

God gave us
two ears and
one mouth
so we may
listen twice as
long as
we speak.

Minutes at the
table don't put
on weight-

it's the seconds.

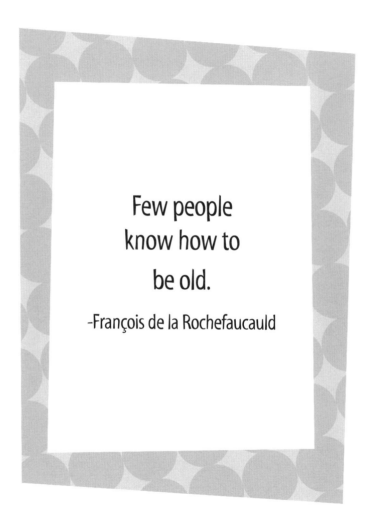

Few people
know how to
be old.

-François de la Rochefaucauld

I quite love
my present age* -
the compensations,
the advantages of it -
the simplifications of freedom,
independence, memories.
But I don't keep it long enough.
It passes too quickly.

- Henry James

* He was 56 at the time.

Being diagnosed
with memory loss
isn't the worst thing
that can happen to you
because in fifteen minutes,
you'll have forgotten
all about it.

An elderly gent was
happily driving along
when he heard a
news bulletin on the radio
warning drivers to avoid
a car traveling in the
wrong direction
on the freeway.
"Hmmph,"
the man snorted,
"looks to me like the
freeway's full of 'em."

All the best sands
of my life are
somehow getting into
the wrong end of
the hourglass.
If I could only reverse it!
Were it in my power
to do so, would I?

- Thomas Bailey Aldrich

For a free facelift,
Smile.

Yoga Class

If I was meant
to do this,
I'd have been
born with
cooked noodles
for legs.

When there's
a long row to hoe,
remember:
God's still in charge
of the garden.

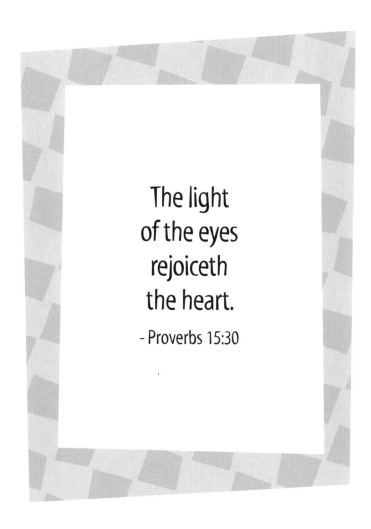

The light
of the eyes
rejoiceth
the heart.

- Proverbs 15:30

We make a living
by what we get,
but we make a life
by what we give.

-Winston Churchill

I am old,
yet I look at wise men
and see that I am very young.
I look over those stars yonder, and
into the myriads of the aspirant and
ordered souls,
and see I am a stranger
and a youth and have yet
my spurs to win.
Too ridiculous
are these airs of age.

- Ralph Waldo Emerson

When I'm tempted
to laugh at someone else,
I just look into the mirror
and find all the
material I need.

Anyone who stops
learning is old,
whether 20 or 80.
Anyone who keeps
learning stays young.
The greatest thing
in life is to keep
your mind young.

- Henry Ford

Age is an
issue of mind
over matter.
If you don't mind,
it doesn't matter.

- Mark Twain

As I approve
of a Youth that has
something of the
Old Man in him,
so I am no less
pleased with an Old Man
that has something
of the Youth.

- Cicero

I want to be thoroughly
used up when I die,
for the harder I work
the more I live.
I rejoice in life for its own sake.
Life is no brief candle to me.
It is a sort of splendid torch
which I've got to hold up
for the moment,
and I want to make it burn
as brightly as possible
before handing it on
to future generations.

- George Bernard Shaw

If you cheat
on your diet,
you'll gain
in the end.

When God looks
for value,
He assesses
what's in the heart,
not what's in
the bank account.

You're
only young
once –
but you can
be immature
forever!

Youth is a
wonderful thing.
What a crime
to waste it
on children.

- George Bernard Shaw

US

• • • • • • • • • • •

When we were growing up, we rarely strayed far from each other. We moved to the same songs, adopted the same styles, and used the same expressions in the firm and unshakeable belief that we were, each of us, a model of individuality.

Now we've arrived at an age where we might, in fact, possess a modicum of individuality. Our beliefs and values have withstood the test of our specific circumstances, our various hopes and dreams have confronted the hard cold facts of life, and our separate careers and interests have shaped us into who we are today, each of us with a unique story to tell. But what's the first thing we think when those first wrinkles emerge, when those heretofore limber knee joints start to creak? "Oh no! Am I the only one who…? Am I the only one that…?"

The answer is No—a comforting No. We've all counted our gray hairs, felt a spasm of pain along with the exhilaration of winning a weekend basketball game, complained that our grandkids mumble and the newspaper uses smaller print than it used to. We don't need to even imagine we're the only ones. In fact, let's at last celebrate (and give thanks for) the way it's always been: We're all in this together!

• • • • • • • • • • •

Count yourself
blessed
every day
and you will
find yourself living
in a world
of blessings.

In the doctor's office,
a physician asked his
patient, an eighty-nine-year
old woman, how she felt
getting up in the morning.
"Surprised," she replied,
"very surprised."

I Have Seen

• • • • • • • • • • •

Lord, I have seen your work in my life. From birth you brought me safely through childhood, and you led me through the traumas of my teen years, picking me up and dusting me off when I stumbled and fell (more times than I care to admit).

Though I didn't realize it when I was twenty, thirty, or forty, you sent friends and family to encourage me through the rough spots of life and celebrate with me when times were good. Looking back through those years, I see now that all those "lucky breaks" and "happy coincidences" of my life were your hand leading me, your love present in the course of my every day.

So why should I be afraid of turning fifty, sixty, seventy, eighty, or ninety? Do I think you, eternal God, have never seen a wrinkle on a human face or laid eyes on a gray hair, or you, ever-present God, give up on people when they can no longer do the things they used to do? Have I ever seen you abandon your loved ones?

No, Lord, that's not what I've seen. Instead, I've seen you smooth the lines of faces once worn with worry, and I've seen you fill with joy hearts once weighted down with grief. I've seen a young spirit dance in the eyes of elderly women and the smile of peace warm the face of aged men.

All this Lord, I have seen...and that's why I have no fear of anything the years ahead may bring.

• • • • • • • • • •

There is no greater blessing
than a good friend –
except a good friend
who grows to be
an old friend.

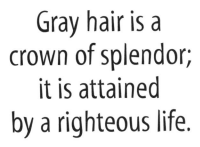

Gray hair is a
crown of splendor;
it is attained
by a righteous life.

- Proverbs 16:31 (NIV)

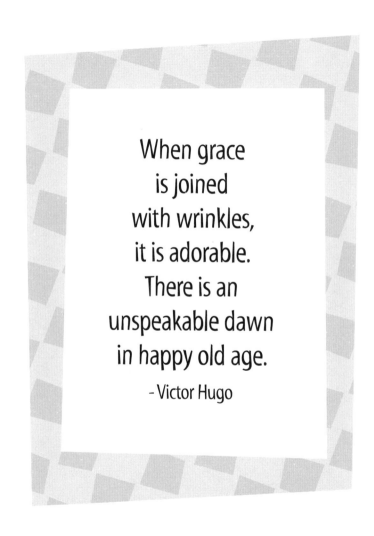

When grace
is joined
with wrinkles,
it is adorable.
There is an
unspeakable dawn
in happy old age.

- Victor Hugo

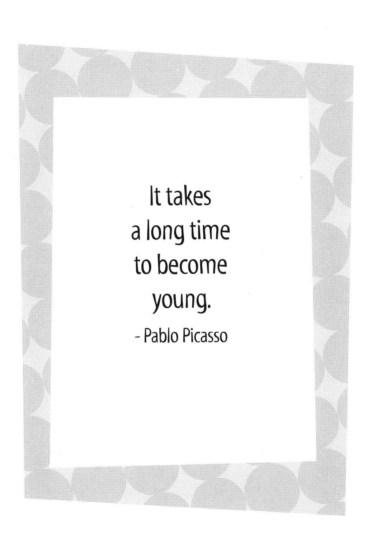

It takes
a long time
to become
young.

- Pablo Picasso

Give your spirit
something to
smile about...
count your
blessings.

DON'T WAIT
TO FIND LIFE
WORTH LIVING –
MAKE IT
THAT WAY.

If you want to
find out how
rich you are,
count all the
things you have
that money
can't buy.

The art of
being wise
is the art
of knowing what
to overlook.

-William James

Dear God,
do you
really make
angels...
or just
grandparents?

On the patio of a nursing home, two elderly women were sitting in their rocking chairs and reminiscing. "All my friends are long gone," one sighed. "I guess St. Peter has forgotten all about me." The other woman quickly looked around. Seeing no one, she turned to her companion "Shhhhh!" she said, putting her finger to her lips.

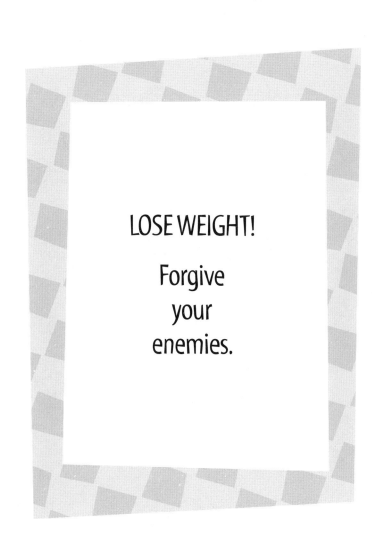

LOSE WEIGHT!

Forgive
your
enemies.

Smile
and the world
smiles
with you;
snore
and you sleep alone.

Age is opportunity no less
Than youth itself,
though in another dress,
And as the evening
twilight fades away
The sky is filled with stars,
invisible by day.

- Henry Wadsworth Longfellow

It doesn't feel good
when you realize
you pay more for a
postage stamp today
than it used to cost
to see a matinee movie.

Preferred Definitions

NO:	YES:
Wrinkles	Laugh lines
Gray hair	Symbol of authority
Sagging anatomy	Fresh new body configuration
Slowing down	Living mindfully
Hard of hearing	Selective listening
Senior moment	Innovative response to a given situation
Mind gone blank	Moment of deep reflection
Forgetful	Able to let go of the past
Aging hippie	Person who possesses a youthful spirit
Geezer rocker crooning an old hit	Entertainer who knows good music
Old stuff	Collectors' items worth a lot of money
Old story repeated a dozen times	Wisdom gained from long experience
The way they do it now	The right way

God's
Office
Hours:
24/7

In a changing world,
one thing is always certain:
I'll end up in the check-out lane
that comes to a standstill.

Art is in the eye of the beholder

● ● ● ● ● ● ● ● ● ●

I was in the grocery store standing in line at the check stand the other day behind a lovely young woman wearing a tank top and shorts. Across her shoulders and snaking down her firm tanned arms was an elegantly drawn, brightly colored tattoo. I had to wonder: Do kids nowadays know that the law of gravity applies to body parts, too?

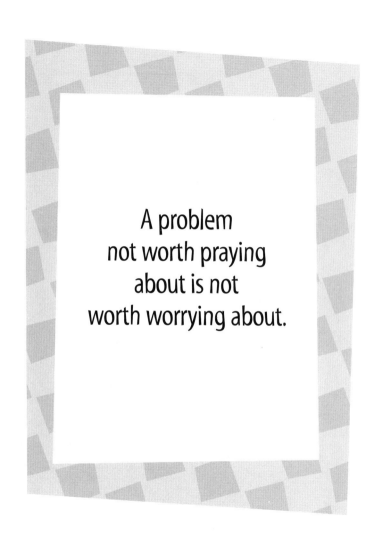

A problem
not worth praying
about is not
worth worrying about.

The Blessing
of Old Friends...
can't be counted in cups of coffee
or hours spent together
but by the deep and constant
certainty that
someone cares.

Do not grow old,
no matter how
long you live.
Never cease to stand
like curious children
before the Great Mystery
into which we are born.

- Albert Einstein

A heart filled
with gratitude
has no room
for despair.

The Best View of the Blooms

• • • • • • • • • • •

A young woman was jogging through her neighborhood past a house with an exception-ally well-kept and attractive garden. Slowing down to admire the profusion of colorful and fragrant blooms on stems peeking through the yard's neat picket fence, the jogger spied an elderly woman kneeling in one of the beds.

The jogger stopped. "Good morning," she called to the gardener. "I just want to say how much I admire your garden!"

"Well," the elderly woman frowned as she pulled herself up, "it's getting harder and harder to take care of, you know."

"But you do a beautiful job," the jogger said.

"Not like I used to." The woman shook her head and frowned. "My arthritis kicks in and I just can't get to everything I want to do. You should have seen it twenty years ago."

The young woman persisted in her praise for the gardener whose handiwork brightened the whole block.

The gardener, not to be budged from her negative attitude, continued to air her complaints. Finally the jogger broke in. "Well, you have to admit," she said with a smile, "it's better to be up here on earth looking down on the flowers than to be under the earth staring up at their roots!"

• • • • • • • • • •

The trouble
with being old
enough to have
some answers is
that no one is
asking you
any questions.

I remember
when sitting
on the front porch
and watching
cars go by
occupied the
entire family
for a whole
evening.

Old wood best to burn,
old wine to drink,
old friends to trust,
and old authors to read.

- Francis Bacon

We're not
forgetful–

We simply choose
to ignore
all the stupid
things we used
to know.

You know you're
getting older
when what you
wore in your
twenties
is back in style –
again.

Look on the
bright side:
When you're the
only one of your
contemporaries still
living, you can finally
forget about
peer pressure.

IF YOUR MIND
GOES BLANK,
BE SURE
TO TURN OFF
THE SOUND.

Worrying
is paying
for trouble
you don't
have.

Since I know that God
will let me live long enough to
accomplish all the tasks
He has put me on earth to do,
I'll just sit here and relax.
After all, there's no sense
hurrying to get things done.

Let's thank God because...

if the church roof leaks,
no one expects us to climb up and fix it...

if the sermon puts us to sleep,
we can blame the medication we're on...

if we've never liked going to evening
meetings, we can tell them
we can't drive after dark anymore...

if we don't remember the names
of people we see every Sunday,
we can just smile and say,
"You know, I'm not getting any younger"
(thank God!).

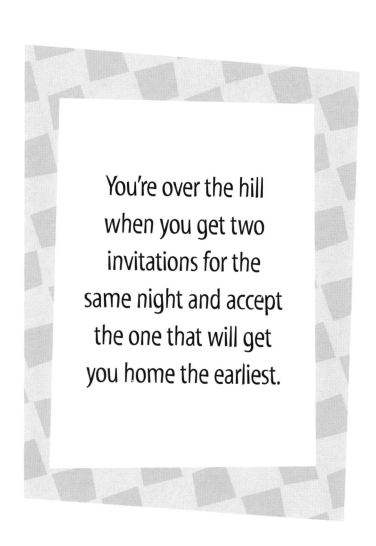

You're over the hill when you get two invitations for the same night and accept the one that will get you home the earliest.

Party Party Party
ALL NIGHT LONG!

Or at least until 8:30.

Store the ice cream in the oven.

Enter your PIN into the microwave.

Nag your adult children
about anything.

Insist someone stole your car, only
to remember you took the bus.

Observe a stranger's tattoo
and criticize it—loudly.

Run to answer the cuckoo clock.

Make small talk with yourself.

Open a can of soup when
you meant to fry an egg.

Maintain you're right—
whether you're right or not.

Enter a room, then ask yourself
why you're there.

Name all your prescriptions whenever
anyone asks, "How are you?"

Thank the Lord your senior moments
are what they are—moments!

We know
we're getting old
when we can't
do one thing...

without first
remembering
how it USED
to be done.

After a certain age,
you don't bother
holding your
stomach in,
no matter
who's looking
at you.

The aging process
would sure slow down
if it had to work its way
through Congress.

An Elderly Man

• • • • • • • • • •

An elderly man and his wife, married 60 years and in good health because of the wife's insistence on healthy eating, died together in a car crash. They stepped into heaven together and were greeted by St. Peter, who began showing them around their new home. The couple was astounded at heaven's beauty. They were thrilled to meet their friends who had passed away before them. "This is truly paradise!" the wife exclaimed.

Just then, the husband spied a splendid golf course.

"How much are the green fees?" the man asked St. Peter.

"Like everything else here, it's free," St. Peter replied. "You can play whenever you like."

Angrily, the man turned to his wife. "If it weren't for you making me eat broccoli," he growled, "I could have been here years ago!"

When you can
laugh at yourself,
you're never at a
loss for humor.

If you can't
thank God for what
you have,
thank Him
for what
you have
escaped.

A clear
conscience
is a
soft bed.

Grandpa watched
as his grandson downloaded
video after video onto a flash drive.
Impressed, Grandpa said,
"I wish I could store
information like that."
"You always have,"
his wife called from
the kitchen.
"It's just you can't
retrieve it like you used to."

Two Sisters

• • • • • • • • • •

Two sisters, both in their sixties, held different opinions on whether or not a woman's gray hair should be colored. "It looks old," claimed the elder of the two, who began coloring her hair decades earlier and continued to do so.

"I think it looks distinguished," demurred the younger, who had let nature take its course.

"No," the elder sneered. "More like extinguished."

Times sure change...

Somewhere
along the way,
things went
from Flower Power
to Power Naps.

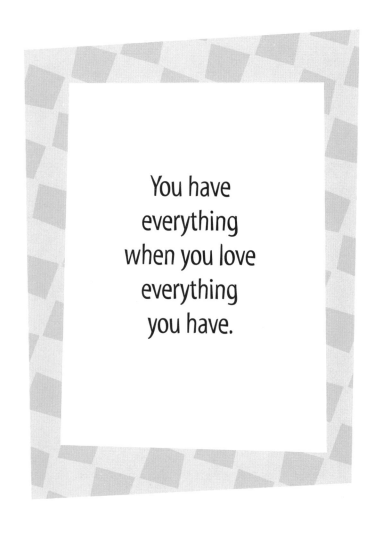

You have
everything
when you love
everything
you have.

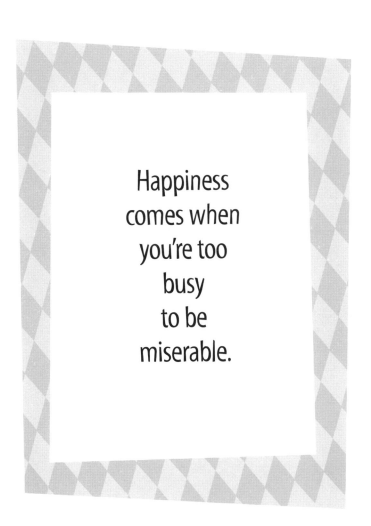

Happiness
comes when
you're too
busy
to be
miserable.

A Question

Dear God, I have to ask
about that thing called time,
Because it up and left me
somewhat past my prime.

Today, the mirror showed
a head of graying hair,
A face with lines and wrinkles,
chin, and chin to spare!

How did those years become
a part of history?
What happened to the youngster
I still see as me?

Dear God, I have to ask!

You know you're
getting old when
it's not the food itself
you talk about,
but whether you're supposed
to take your pills with it.

Every Day, Lord

Every day, Lord help me to live
in a way that is pleasing to you.
From the sparkle of dawn
to the tranquility of eventide
May my thoughts be true and loving,
My words pure and honorable,
and may everything I do
be to your glory.
A-men.

Bless Me, Lord

Oh Lord, where have the seasons gone?
It seems "my day" was long before
the kids today were born.

I'm thankful I can rise from bed,
But every bone aches, groans, and creaks,
And things that I know how to use
I buy in stores that sell antiques.

Of course, I know that youth—
That season in the sun—
was never meant to last,
But bless me, Lord, I sure do wish
it hadn't gone so fast!

Today
was once
the FUTURE
from which you
expected so much
in the past.

If you want
to know what
heaven looks like,
make someone smile.

A young boy's eyes widened
as the candles were lighted
on his great-grandmother's
birthday cake. "How old is
Great-Grandma?"
he whispered to his mother.
"Your great-grandma is one
hundred years old today,"
his mother said proudly.
"Wow." Seeing all the candles aglow,
he turned to his sister and said,
"It's no wonder they talk
about global warming."

Old age
is when it takes
longer to rest
than to get tired.

A guy knows
he's old
when he's
cautioned
to slow down
by his doctor
instead of
the police.

The best thing
about recalling
our crazy old times...

is how much
it embarrasses
the kids!

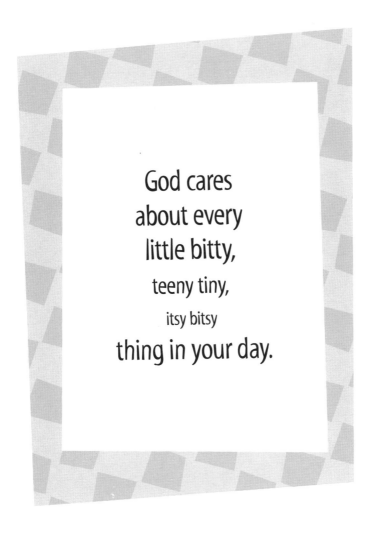

God cares
about every
little bitty,
teeny tiny,
itsy bitsy
thing in your day.

There's no such thing as an ordinary day to those that look at it in an extraordinary way.

Sometimes miracles
fall from heaven...
but most of the time,
they're right
at our feet.

You know you've
been out of touch
with the music world
for a long time
when the oldies station
is playing songs
you've never heard
in the first place.